Fester the Pester

To Kendall!

Publisher's Cataloging-In-Publication
(Provided by Quality Books, Inc.)

Finklea, Michael, 1962-
    Fester the Pester / written by Michael Finklea ;
illustrated by Vickie Sissel. – 1st ed.
    p. cm.
    SUMMARY : Fester the Pester is a little chigger who
can really get under your skin! Fester learns that his
teasing doesn't get him anywhere when he meets the new
student in school, Debramacdoogle Spidernoodle. Usually
when Fester gets a reaction out of the other students,
he continues to tease them. But when Debramacdoogle
refuses to react to Fester's repeated attempts to tease
her, he leaves her alone.
    Audience: Elementary school children.
    ISBN 1-931650-01-2

    1. Chiggers (Mites)--Juvenile fiction. 2. Teasing--
Juvenile fiction. 3. Conduct of life--Juvenile fiction.
[1. Chiggers (Mites)--Fiction. 2. Teasing--Fiction.
3. Conduct of life--Fiction. 4. Stories in rhyme.]
I. Sissel, Vickie, ill. II. Title.

PZ8.3.F623Fes 2001   [E]
               QBI01-700692

Fester the Pester

Written by
Michael Finklea

Illustrated by
Vickie Sissel

Coastal Publishing
1025C W. 5th North Street
Summerville, SC. 29483
843-875-7775

Dedicated to Debra Morris Gibbs

You have inspired me many times in so many ways!
The character, Debramacdoogle Spidernoodle, was inspired after
listening to your wonderful stories of growing up being teased from
having beautiful red hair. **Kids will be kids.** It is too bad they do not
always understand that their teasing can really hurt.   Thank you for all of
the encouragement you have given me throughout the years. You are a true friend!

A member of the Kentucky Library Association: A major advocate of the Accelerated
Reader Program: Your dedication to children's literature has reached over 30,000
students during the past 20 years. They have all been truly blessed .
Kindergarten student, Kristin Caudill, read over
330 books reaching 157.1 AR points –
That is something to celebrate!

– About the author –
Michael travels to elementary schools at no charge and can be contacted at 800-371--7709.

Other books in print!
Good-Natured Nina the Nervous Gnat - a rhyming book promoting better character traits.
Good-Natured Nina the Nervous Gnat (The Sports Edition) - includes sports themes and the importance of teamwork.
The Worldwide Adventures of Winston & Churchill (Europe) - a tour through Europe with two adventurous mice.
Who Are You Calling Junior? - try and figure out what the animal is with clues. Facts section included.

Soon to be released!
Jeepers Creepers (Two Tales of Horror!)

Meet Fester the pester

Does Fester get under your skin
Like when he teases the others?
If it doesn't bother you
Then he will pester another!

It's what he does best —
Make you itch when he pesters,
For it is his hobby.
They call him the tease tester!

"Good morning, class.
I'm Ms. Ima Pheasant.
When I call out your name,
Please answer present."

She called out the names
Spud, Fester, and then Moe.
But when she called out Debramacdoogle,
Fester bit his big toe.

"Yes, I'm Debramacdoogle,"
The new spider said with a smile.
"My last name is Spidernoodle."
Fester fell in the aisle.

Ms. Pheasant then pointed
Right at the door.
"Fester, to the principal you go
After you get off the floor."

As Fester walked down the hall,
He wiped the grin off his face.
For Ms. Pheasant was yelling,
"Boy, you better pick up the pace!"

He was already prepared
And just as slick as a cat,
He began to tell his story
To Ms. Nina the gnat.

"I had to laugh, Ms. Nina,
And I think you'll agree,
For it was my funny bone I hit,"
He started to plea.

"I had to laugh so loud
Till I fell from my seat
And slid to the ground
In a big laughing heap!"

Fester looked up
And thought, yes, in fact,
Ms. Nina believed him again.
And she gave Fester a pat.

"If that is the truth
Then you are not in trouble.
Fester, get back to class,
And I mean on the double."

Fester left Principal Nina
In a big blaze of dust.
He had to find Debramacdoogle.
This was a must!

Back down the hall,
It was Cheetah he saw.
He tied a string on his tail.
Now he got ole southpaw!

It really wasn't a bore.
Nothing excited him more
Than to pester the others
And watch the tears pour.

He may not have many friends.
For this he can't grin.
But who cares? Batty Betty
Is alone in the gym!

So, to the gym he scurried
In a little bit of a hurry.
He had to get back to class
To avoid any worry.

"Hey there, Batty Betty . . .
Are you acting your age?
Or I think they will put you
In a batty bird cage!"

Betty turned to him.
She started to screech,
"That bothers me, Fester.
Why are you so mean?"

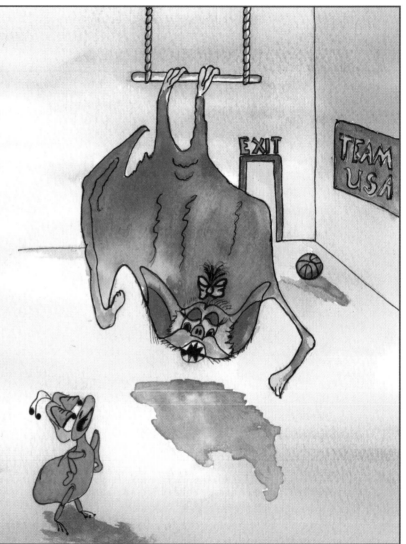

Another one down.
He got her to frown.
He's a little chigger who thinks
He ought to be wearing a crown!

For if Fester knows
He can get to them,
His teases will work
And then he will win.

Later that day
Fester sat down to lunch
And saw Debramacdoogle
Starting to munch.

It's time for his rhyme,
And he follows his hunch.
It will embarrass her
In front of the bunch.

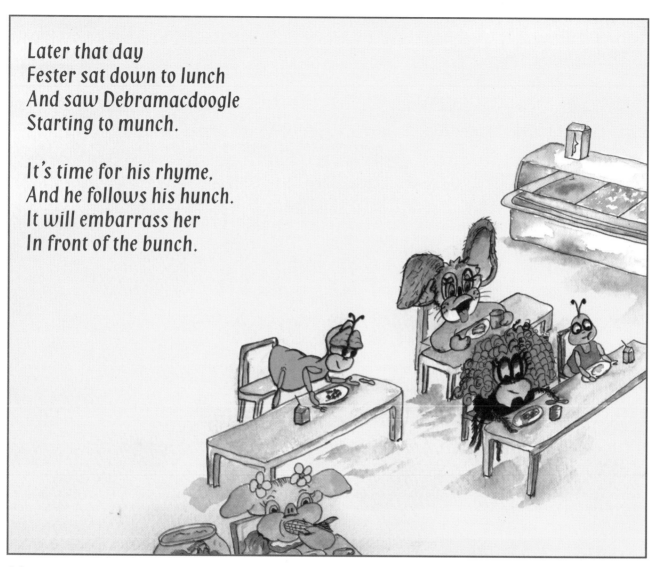

"Hey look, everyone.
There's Debramacdoogle.
She is as thin as her web,
A real spider noodle.

With that head of curls
She eats apple strudel.
A spider she's not.
I think she's a poodle!"

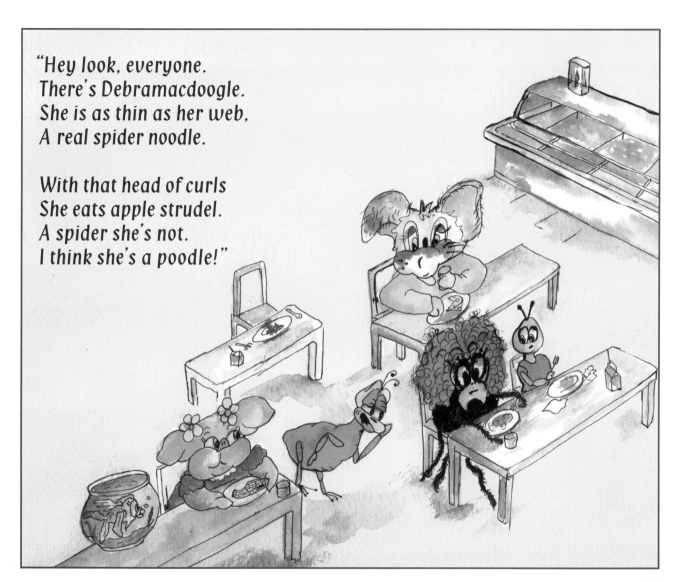

17

Deb just glanced up at him,
Then went back to her plate.
This was something
Fester really did hate!

"Did you hear what I said,
Debramacdoogle?
I said that you looked like
You may be part poodle."

But Debramacdoogle didn't say a word
About the rhyme he had sprung.
He wondered, what's wrong?
Maybe a cat got her tongue?

So Fester turned back to Dell
And said, "What's this I smell?"
Dell broke down in tears.
His tease worked like a spell.

There was complete silence,
Then everyone laughed.
With Ms. Pheasant not present,
Fester blazed a new path.

But it really bothered Fester
About Debramacdoogle.
Why didn't she respond
When he called her a poodle?

Fester had to find her
To make her agree
That his pestering worked
When he came to Bailey.

Bailey was sitting
On top of her drum.
She had been paying attention.
A good listener she'd become.

Bailey remarked, "I heard what you said,
And I'll be very exact.
Debra doesn't care what you say.
This may be a fact."

The whole next week
Fester spent spinning his web,
It was a cobweb that caught him,
Spun by little ole Deb.

"Fester, it doesn't bother me
What you have said.
Besides, if I get mad at you,
It is your thrill I have fed.

I am proud of who I am
For I am unique!
There is not another like me.
I may be small, but I'm not weak.

It is as simple as that.
I refuse to react.
But have you really thought
Of your teasing impact?

Why not make friends?
For the teasing won't win
When you start to understand
We all want the same from within."

Fester decided to leave
Debramacdoogle alone.
His teasing didn't work
For this she had shown.

So he will continue to tease,
But remember this fact.
The only reason he does
Is because they react.

It wasn't long after that
Fester was pulled out of math.
Like a lonely cowboy he walked
Back into Ms. Nina's warpath!